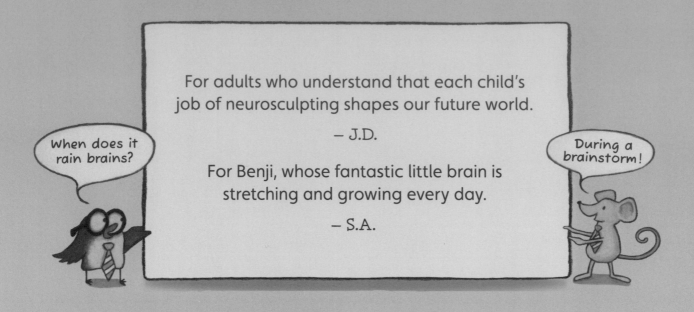

For adults who understand that each child's job of neurosculpting shapes our future world.
— J.D.

For Benji, whose fantastic little brain is stretching and growing every day.
— S.A.

When does it rain brains?

During a brainstorm!

Library of Congress Cataloging-in-Publication Data is available.
Library of Congress Catalog Card Number 2010913850

ISBN 978-0-9829938-0-4

13 12 11 10 09   1 2 3 4 5 6 7 8 9 10

Printed in Canada
First edition 2010

Little Pickle Press LLC
PO Box 983
Belvedere, CA 94920

Please visit us at www.littlepicklepress.com.

Your FANTASTIC ELASTIC BRAIN

Stretch It, Shape It

By
JoAnn Deak, Ph.D.

Little Pickle Press

Illustrated by
Sarah Ackerley

What does your **BRAIN** *really* do?

Does it fill the space between your ears?

Well yes . . . but your brain can do so much more!

Your brain helps you **think** . . .
and **remember** . . .

Good kitty.

and name what you **see** . . .
and what you **hear** . . .

It lets you move your body . . .
and **feel**—both touch
and emotions.

So what is your brain? Is it a muscle?
No, the brain is an organ in your body.
It's made up of cells and tissue.

The brain controls everything you do,
everything you think, everything you feel . . .
even everything you dream.

The brain has many parts that do all kinds of different jobs.

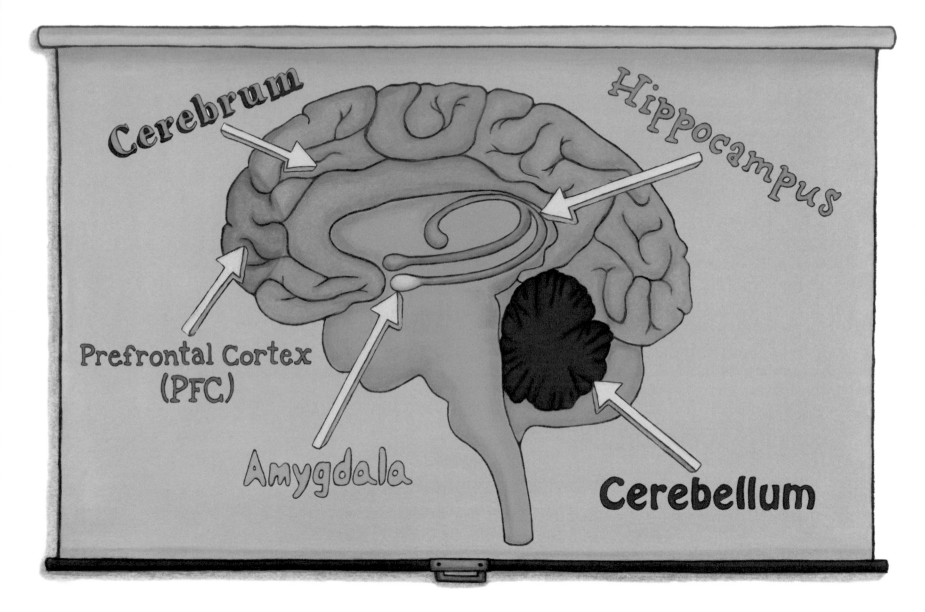

Cerebrum

(suh-REE-bruhm)

The **Cerebrum** is the largest part of your brain. It helps you think and speak.

Cerebellum (SAIR-uh-bel-uhm)

The **Cerebellum** is a small part at the back of the brain that helps your muscles to coordinate your movement and your balance, so that you can walk, ride a bike, or play tag.

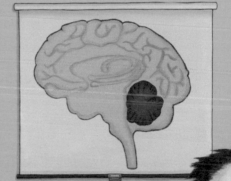

Prefrontal Cortex

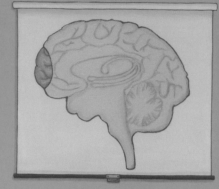

The **Prefrontal Cortex** (PFC, for short) is the part of your brain behind your forehead. It lets you make plans and decisions.

Hippocampus

(hip-uh-KAM-pus)

The **Hippocampus** is at the center of your brain. It works like a file cabinet to help you store and find memories.

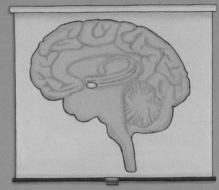

Amygdala

(uh-MIG-duh-luh)

The **Amygdala** is a tightly-packed group of cells deep within the center of the brain that controls your emotions.

Excited

Angry

Embarrassed

Frightened

Sad

Happy

Neurons

(NER-onz)

Neurons are everywhere in your brain. They are tiny brain cells that make electrical signals to send messages to other cells in your body telling them what to do.

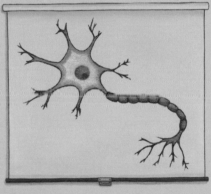

Amygdala means "almond."
(amygdala)

I can see how it got that name.
(almond)

When you were born, you were very little.
Your brain was small and not so strong.

As you get older . . .  your body grows
and gets stronger.

As part of your body, your brain grows,
and learns to do new things.

And you can make your brain do even more!

Your brain grows very fast during the first ten years of your life. This is the *magic decade* when you can help your brain grow *faster* . . . and be more *powerful*. Just like lifting weights helps your muscles get *stronger* . . . learning new things strengthens your brain. You can give your brain a good workout by trying to learn many different things.

Like elastic bands that

S-T-R-E-T-C-H

when you pull them . . .

even things that
are hard at first . . .

or that you don't
like to do . . .

or that you don't do very well . . .

Nice kick!

get easier when
you keep trying.

Think about
the first time you
played soccer. You
probably couldn't kick
the ball far or make many
goals. But as you kept going
to practices, you learned
more about the rules of the
game and followed your
coach's directions.

The muscles in your legs
and feet got stronger, your
movements were more
coordinated, and you could
run farther and faster.

Learning more and
practicing what you learned
let you play better and
have more fun.

*Practice really does
make perfect . . .
or, at least, much better!*

Even when you make a mistake while you're learning something new . . .

you are still training your brain.

You will remember that mistake and try something else—until you get it right.

Making mistakes is one of the best ways your brain learns and grows.

If you aren't willing to risk being wrong, you won't take the chances that S-T-R-E-T-C-H your elastic brain.

You can stretch the part of your brain that controls your feelings, too.

If you are frightened about taking a risk, like learning to swim, finding the courage to put your face in the water S-T-R-E-T-C-H-E-S your amygdala. It will remind you that you overcame your fear . . .

so you will be braver the next time something scares you— like diving into the water.

Learning something new causes the brain to grow more connections among the neurons.

With more connections, the neurons can send and receive more messages.

These connections help to stretch a part of your brain and make it more elastic, so that it can hold more information and ideas.

How does the brain stretch and grow?

Neuro- means that the word it is part of has something to do with the brain.

A **sculptor** molds, shapes, or carves things out of clay, or wood, or stone.

So, you shape your brain when you make it bigger by adding new things you know and can do.

You are a Neurosculptor!

How did you *do* that?

Neurons, my feathered friend.

In the same way that the muscles in your body work together when you want to lift a heavy object or kick a ball, the different parts of your brain work together when you're learning something new.

The amygdala makes you want to learn to play the piano.

The cerebrum helps you decide to practice.

The cerebellum calls up the memory of watching and listening when your piano teacher showed you how to play a new piece of music. Then, your cerebellum sends messages through neurons to the muscles in your wrists, hands, and fingers, so that you can hit the right notes.

The next time you play that piece of music, the parts of your brain and body will know how to work together, and you will play the song more easily.

The brain that makes you YOU  really is an amazing organ! It controls what you think, do, feel, and **remember**. Your brain is growing very fast during your first ten years of life and now we know that you can help it grow.

When you try hard to learn something new, connections grow from **neurons** and  attach to other **neurons**.

Then, your brain can send messages faster, making part of your brain BIGGER and stronger. Making mistakes really helps you learn, because your brain keeps trying new things and S-T-R-E-T-C-H-I-N-G until you figure out the answer to your problem. You are shaping a more elastic brain when you learn new things that build on what you already know.

The more different kinds of things you learn and think about, the more you can learn, know, and enjoy.

The harder you try without giving up, the more you will learn.

You really can train your brain to be fit and strong and to keep stretching and growing throughout your whole life!

Our Mission

Little Pickle Press is dedicated to helping parents and educators cultivate conscious, responsible little people by stimulating explorations of the meaningful topics of their generation through a variety of media, technologies, and techniques.

Little Pickle Press
Environmental Benefits Statement

TerraSkin® paper is a revolutionary new paper made from stone. Infinitely recyclable and degradable, it requires no water, no bleach, and uses 50% less energy and 20–30% less ink than traditional paper in the manufacturing and printing process. Along with all of these sustainable advantages, this environmentally-friendly, tree-less paper is water-resistant and durable with a unique texture and feel that produces beautiful printing results that equal or exceed that of fiber paper while protecting the Earth's precious resources.

Little Pickle Press saved the following resources by using TerraSkin paper:

trees	wastewater	energy	solid waste	greenhouse gases
76	**29,558**	**26**	**2,595**	**7,892**
Fully Grown	Gallons	Million BTUs	Pounds	Pounds

Calculations based on research by Environmental Defense Fund and other members of the Paper Task Force.

We print and distribute our materials in an environmentally-friendly manner, using recycled paper, soy inks, and green packaging.

www.littlepicklepress.com

About the Author

JoAnn Deak, Ph.D., is an author and an international speaker, educator, and preventive psychologist. She also works with parents, teachers and other adults who work with children as a consultant to schools worldwide on issues of brain development and gender equity.

About the Illustrator

Sarah Ackerley began pursuing her dream of becoming a real live picture book illustrator after earning her BFA from the University of Texas at Austin in 2004. To her delight, Sarah currently works as an illustrator in Los Altos, California, where she resides with her husband and two fickle cats. Visit Sarah on the web at www.sarahackerley.com.